C·3

Fact Finders®

EXTREME LIFE

Scaly Blood Squirters

AND OTHER EXTREME REPTILES

BY JUNE PRESZLER

Consultant:
The Staff of Reptile Gardens
Rapid City, South Dakota

Capstone press®

Mankato, Minnesota

Fact Finders are published by Capstone Press,
151 Good Counsel Drive, P.O. Box 669, Mankato, Minnesota 56002.
www.capstonepress.com

Library of Congress Cataloging-in-Publication Data
Preszler, June, 1954–
    Scaly blood squirters and other extreme reptiles / by June Preszler.
    p. cm — (Fact finders. Extreme life)
    Summary: "Describes the world of reptiles, including characteristics, life cycles, and
defenses" — Provided by publisher.
    Includes bibliographical references and index.
    ISBN–13: 978–1–4296–1269–2 (hardcover)
    ISBN–10: 1–4296–1269–X (hardcover)
    1. Lizards — Juvenile literature. 2. Reptiles — Juvenile literature. I. Title. II. Series.
QL666.L2P74 2008
597.9 — dc22   2007026967

Editorial Credits
Megan Schoeneberger and Lori Shores, editors; Alison Thiele, designer and illustrator;
    Linda Clavel, photo researcher

Photo Credits
Animals Animals/Earth Scenes/JOE MC DONALD, 28; Zigmund Leszczynski, 25
Ardea/Jean Paul Ferrero, 23; John Cancalosi, 5, 18; M. Watson, 13
Bruce Coleman Inc./Erwin & Peggy Bauer, 15
Corbis/Gallo Images, 11; Rod Patterson, 9 (bottom); Jonathan Blair, 22 (top)
Dwight R. Kuhn, 26
Jacob Goldfarb, cover
Jupiterimages, 7 (top left)
Nature Picture Library/Anup Shah, 17
Peter Arnold/A.Visage, 19
Photo Researchers, Inc/SPL/John Devries, 10
Scott Thoms, 9 (top)
Shutterstock/EcoPrint, 7 (bottom right); John Bell, 7 (middle), JOSE ALBERTO TEJO, 7 (bottom left);
    Mike Grindley, 21; Steve Lovegrove, 24 (top)
Visuals Unlimited/Jack Milchanowski, 16; Jim Merli, 22 (bottom), 24 (bottom); Tom J. Ulrich, 7 (top
    right)

1 2 3 4 5 6 13 12 11 10 09 08

TABLE OF CONTENTS

CHAPTER 1

THE TRUTH ABOUT REPTILES

A hungry coyote scans the landscape. All he sees is sand, rocks, and thorny bushes. Every so often, an ant scurries past.

Suddenly, one of the rocks shoots out a sticky tongue and nabs an ant.

Wait just a second. That's no rock. It's a horned lizard!

The coyote moves closer. The lizard gulps in air and puffs up its body like a prickly balloon. All at once, its eyelids swell shut. Bright red blood shoots from the corner of one eye and into the coyote's mouth. Startled, the coyote runs away.

The coyote doesn't know that the horned lizard only looks tough. It's actually a very harmless little creature, unless you're a bug. Horned lizards love to eat bugs!

The horned lizard looks a bit like a toad. Some people even call them horny toads. But horned lizards aren't toads at all. They are one of about 8,000 kinds of reptiles.

And What, Exactly, Are Reptiles?

Let's step back for just a moment. Scientists have seen, studied, and named millions of animals on the planet. And they're not done yet. To keep all the animals straight, scientists sort all living things into groups based on shared features. Reptiles make up one of these groups.

So what features do all reptiles have in common? All reptiles have backbones and dry, **scaly** skin. They are all cold-blooded, which means that their body temperature changes with their surroundings.

Scientists split the big group of reptiles into smaller groups called familes. They compare features like body shape, eyelids, and ear openings. They also note whether or not the reptile has a shell. The smallest groups within families are called **species**.

scaly: covered with small bits of hard skin called scales

species: a specific type of animal, insect, or plant

REPTILE FAMILIES

no legs

long, thin body and tail

SNAKE

LIZARD

four legs

SNAKES AND LIZARDS
- at least 4,500 species of lizards
- about 3,000 species of snakes
- live mostly in warm places

TUATARAS
- two species
- live on islands off the coast of New Zealand

TUATARA

looks like a lizard, but related to dinosaurs

powerful tail

ALLIGATOR

CROCODILIANS
- at least 20 species
- includes alligators, caimans, gavials, and crocodiles
- live in or near bodies of water

webbed hind feet

long snout

TURTLES AND TORTOISES
- about 300 species
- live on land, in fresh water, and in salt water

shell

TORTOISE

CHAPTER 2

Weird, Wonderful Reptiles

If you've seen one reptile, you've seen them all, right? No way! Reptiles come in every size and shape. Some reptiles are bright blue, yellow, or purple. Some reptiles, such as the paradise tree snake, glide through treetops. They can shoot blood, like horned lizards. Or they can spit **venom**, like the African spitting cobra. In fact, the reptile family is full of oddballs.

Are softshelled turtles missing their shells? Not really. A turtle's shell is formed by flat bones attached to its back and ribs. In most turtles, those bones are covered with big, hard scales. But softshelled turtles have leathery skin covering their bones instead.

venom: a poisonous liquid made by some snakes

WEiRD!

Softshelled turtles have long, round noses. They use their noses like snorkels to breathe when they swim underwater.

The African spitting cobra can spit venom as far as 6.5 feet (2 meters).

Other Strange Reptiles

A few lizard species don't have any legs. They look like fat snakes. But if you get a close look at one, you'll see that it has eyelids. Most lizards have eyelids and can blink. Snakes can't blink. Instead of eyelids, they have permanent see-through scales that cover their eyes.

It might look like a snake, but this slowworm is a lizard!

Geckos are lizards that don't have eyelids. When a gecko gets dust in its eyes, it just flicks its long skinny tongue out and up. Like windshield wipers on a dirty car, the gecko cleans off its eyes.

Speaking of eyes, some reptiles have an extra one. A young tuatara's third eye sits on the top of its head. It is not used for seeing, but it can tell light and dark. Skin covers the eye of adult tuataras.

SUPER-SIZED! TOP 5 BIG REPTILES

① Saltwater crocodiles are the largest reptiles. They usually grow to about 16 feet (5 meters) long. Some have been reported to grow to 20 feet (6 meters) long.

② Komodo dragons are the largest lizards. They can weigh as much as 300 pounds (136 kilograms). That's more than the combined weight of three typical 10-year-old kids.

③ Leatherback sea turtles are the largest turtles. Their shells can be up to 8 feet (2.4 meters) long.

④ The Galapagos tortoise is the largest tortoise. It can weigh up to a whopping 600 pounds (272 kilograms)!

⑤ Anacondas are the heaviest snakes. These heavyweights can weigh up to 500 pounds (227 kilograms).

Tongue-tastic

Lizards and snakes don't use noses to smell like humans do — they use their tongues! Reptiles stick their tongues out to catch scent particles from the air. They transfer these particles to a pit inside their mouths called the Jacobson's organ. The organ detects the smells and alerts them to danger or nearby **prey**.

prey: an animal that is about to be eaten

Fishing, Turtle Style

The matamata turtle from South America has an unusual way of catching fish. Its head and neck are covered by flaps that move in the water. Fish mistake the flaps for plants or other food. When a fish stops for a nibble, the matamata opens its mouth. Swoosh! A rush of water sucks in the tasty little fish.

CHAPTER 3

YOU ARE WHAT YOU EAT

Many people think reptiles are scary. But the truth is that most reptiles are harmless to people. They don't like us, so they stay away. Only Nile crocodiles and saltwater crocodiles sometimes attack people for food.

The animals in real danger are birds, frogs, insects, fish, and deer. These animals are common meals for reptiles. Some lizards and tortoises eat only plants, but most reptiles are **carnivores**. They love meat!

Some reptiles even feast on other reptiles. Tuataras eat smaller lizards. Some snakes, like anacondas and pythons, catch crocodiles and caimans. A Komodo dragon will even eat its own family!

carnivores: meat eaters

anaconda swallowing a caiman

CRAZY!

A dead rattlesnake can bite! Rattlesnake bites have been reported up to an hour after the snake's death.

Snake Snack Attack

Serving Size: Enough for one adult anaconda

Ingredients: One crocodile, pig, antelope, or small deer

Steps:

1. Coil your body around your meat of choice. Squeeze tightly until it stops breathing.

2. Use the stretchy tissue in your jaw to open your mouth wide. Swallow meat headfirst. Do not chew.

3. Move one side of your jaw forward. Then move the other side. Repeat until whole meal has been swallowed.

4. Time needed to consume food varies. Large meals could take many days. If any food begins to rot, puke it out.

15

On the Hunt

There's no such thing as a reptile grocery store. Reptiles have to find their own meals. It's a good thing they have some tricks to help them out.

A chameleon has eyes that can look in opposite directions. When it hunts, one eye watches for bugs. The other eye looks around for danger. When a bug gets close, both eyes focus on it. Zing! The chameleon's sticky tongue snatches the bug.

WEIRD!

A chameleon's tongue is as long as its body.

A crocodile's eyes and nostrils are located on the top of its head. This feature allows crocodiles to hide almost completely underwater. If an animal gets too close, the crocodile lunges and knocks it into the water. The crocodile grabs the animal in its strong jaws. It goes into a death roll, twisting the animal underwater. The death roll continues until the animal becomes too confused to escape and drowns.

Gila monster

Deadly Bites

Some reptiles, such as Gila monsters and Mexican beaded lizards, have nasty bites. When the Gila monster bites, deadly venom flows along grooves in the lizard's teeth. It locks its jaws into the prey and doesn't let go. The venom soaks deep into the wound and kills the animal.

Komodo dragons don't have venom. They don't breathe fire, either. But they still have killer bites. These big lizards have millions of dangerous germs in their mouths. Komodo dragons infect their prey with the deadly germs when they bite. Even if the animal escapes, it will die from infection later.

CHAPTER 4

Survival Tricks

The first reptiles lived about 300 million years ago. About 250 million years ago, dinosaurs came on the scene. These reptiles ruled the earth for millions of years. The dinosaurs died off, but plenty of other reptiles managed to survive.

Some of the best known dinosaurs were fierce hunters, but most were peaceful plant-eaters. Many people think reptiles today are just as scary. But the truth is that most of them are actually peaceful too. They may seem terrifying, but most reptiles would rather not get into a fight. They do their best to stay out of trouble. In fact, they have learned many tricks to hide from danger and survive.

The Tyrannosaurus rex was one scary reptile!

camouflage: a way to blend in with one's surroundings

Many reptiles are **camouflage** experts. The alligator snapper might look like a harmless, moss-covered stone. But don't come too close to this turtle! Its snap can be quick and strong.

Saharan sand vipers use their coloring to trick enemies or prey. The snakes wriggle and bury themselves until only their heads poke out of the sand. Their sandy color makes them hard to see.

frill: a ruffle around the neck

Seeing Is Not Believing

Some reptiles get by on their looks. A bigger, tougher reptile is more likely to be left alone by other animals. The **frilled** lizard makes itself appear larger to scare away enemies. Also called the frill-necked lizard, this trickster has a special fold of skin around its neck. This fold of skin opens like an umbrella. Then the lizard stands up on its back legs and bares its teeth. What a scary show!

Head's up! The Australian thorny devil has a false head. When threatened, the lizard puts its head between its legs. This move exposes an odd hump on the back of its neck. The **predator** mistakes this false head for the lizard's real head.

The hognose snake plays dead. It rolls over onto its back. For added effect, it sometimes even lets its mouth hang open and tongue fall out.

predator: an animal that eats other animals

Between a Rock and a Hard Place

The Africa Tornier's tortoise avoids trouble whenever possible. Since its soft shell won't protect it from enemies, sometimes hiding is the best option. When afraid, the tortoise squeezes itself into a crack between two rocks. It's no wonder this reptile is also called a pancake tortoise! The tortoise then puffs up with air to fill the small space. This way it is hard to see, and even harder to pull out if spotted.

GROSS!

If you catch an anole, beware!
It has one last survival trick. The
anole will poop in your hand. Yuck!

By the Skin of Its Tail

The 14-inch (36-centimeter) green lizard, also
known as an anole, drops off part of its tail when
it feels threatened. The predator chasing the lizard
goes after the wiggly tail. Meanwhile, the rest of
the lizard escapes. In a few weeks, another tail
grows to replace the old one.

INTERVIEW WITH A HORNED LIZARD

INTERVIEWER: It's a dangerous world out there for a lizard. Do you have any advice for young horned lizards?

HORNED LIZARD: Stay hidden. If they can't find us, they can't eat us. Luckily, our dull, dirty-looking colors blend right in with the sand and gravel.

INTERVIEWER: Any other tricks?

HORNED LIZARD: Think big! If you're being swallowed, gulp in air to puff up your body. The animal that's trying to eat you will choke and spit you back out.

INTERVIEWER: And what about your famous blood-squirting trick?

HORNED LIZARD: Every horned lizard knows that squirting blood is a last resort. But if all else fails, start squirting. We can shoot blood up to 3 feet (1 meter) in order to scare away an attacker.

The Road to Survival

Over millions of years, reptiles of all kinds have developed tricks for survival. Some use camouflage, others have venom, others hide and surprise enemies. These creatures have learned to make the most of their skins, eyes, or tails. No wonder they have outlived the dinosaurs!

TRUE LIVES OF SCIENTISTS

Slithering, hissing snakes might make some people squirm. But not **herpetologists**. These scientists love studying snakes. Some herpetologists put their lives on the line to study venomous snakes. Why? To understand venom. Herpetologists want to know how it works and how it can be used to save lives.

herpetologist: a scientist who studies amphibians and reptiles.

From Venom to Antivenom

Out of all 3,000 known snake species, only about 300 are venomous. Still, thousands of people around the world die from venomous snakebites every year. But scientists can use venom to make antivenom to treat most snakebites.

To make antivenom, scientists inject a small amount of venom into another animal, like a horse, sheep, or rabbit. These animals naturally produce chemicals in their blood that fight the venom. Scientists collect blood from the animals, purify it, and store it to treat future snakebite victims.

How to Milk a Snake

To collect venom, herpetologists "milk" snakes. The scientists make the snake bite into a piece of rubber or cloth on top of a glass jar. Then they rub the snake's head to make it release venom. Drops of venom fall into the jar.

GLOSSARY

CAMOUFLAGE (KAM-uh-flahzh) — coloring or covering that makes animals, people, and objects look like their surroundings

CARNIVORE (KAR-nuh-vor) — an animal that eats other animals for food

FRILL (FRIL) — a ruffle around the neck

HERPETOLOGIST (hur-pa-TALL-uh-jist) — a scientist who studies reptiles and amphibians

PREDATOR (PRED-uh-tur) — an animal that hunts and eats other animals for food

PREY (PRAY) — an animal that is hunted by another animal for food

SCALE (SKALE) — one of the small pieces of hard skin covering the body of a fish, snake, or other reptile

SPECIES (SPEE-sheez) — a group of plants or animals that share common characteristics

TORTOISE (TOR-tuhss) — a turtle that lives only on land

VENOM (VEN-uhm) — a poisonous liquid made by some snakes

INTERNET SITES

FactHound offers a safe, fun way to find Internet sites related to this book. All of the sites on FactHound have been researched by our staff.

Here's how:

1. Visit *www.facthound.com*

2. Choose your grade level.

3. Type in this book ID **142961269X** for age-appropriate sites. You may also browse subjects by clicking on letters, or by clicking on pictures and words.

4. Click on the **Fetch It** button.

FactHound will fetch the best sites for you!

READ MORE

Davies, Valerie. *Incredible Reptiles and Amphibians.* Wild Life! Columbus, Ohio: School Specialty, 2006.

Harrison, Paul. *Reptiles.* Up Close. New York: PowerKids Press, 2007.

Pyers, Greg. *Why Am I a Reptile?* Classifying Animals. Chicago: Raintree, 2006.

INDEX